Open Gates

By Anna Cellmer

First published in 2009 in Lulu Publisher

By Anna Cellmer

Copyright Anna Cellmer 2009

annaela3@gmail.com
http://stores.lulu.com/annaela3
https://www.facebook.com/pages/Daily-Crumbs-poetry-collections-by-Anna-Cellmer/152073201656457
https://www.facebook.com/opengatesbyAnnaCellmer
https://www.facebook.com/pages/Beautiful-Stranger-by-Anna-Cellmer/211403929016220
https://www.facebook.com/soundofsilencebyannacellmer
https://www.facebook.com/anna.cellmer
https://www.facebook.com/anna.cellmer.1

Cover picture by Magdalena Szurek, many thanks my friend.

It's for you my love
And because of you
To be continued...

Just came to say that you are beautiful

I can't say yet if I want anything from you
I came here just to say
That you are beautiful
And that I enjoy this that I found
In your world
It's so different from this one I know
Maybe that's why it's so interesting to me
But there is something more in it
I think you are special
You gave me new smiles
You gave me wild dreams
During last night
Because I saw all of you
And I wished to be there too
This image so inspiring as a frightener
But beautiful and sweet the same
What to do if I see only a beauty in you
Maybe we all miss for pain as for love
Maybe we all search for this that we can't find
In this simple world?
Without going a little bit the frames out
We can't really know who we are
I found your world tender, sensual and beautiful
No real brutality is in you even when you give pain is just to feel more
Besides I always believed in the charm of new experiences
As I saw on your site
How enjoyable!
Thank you, one more time to leave me with smile!
And quite excited!
That what it's all about !

The slight difference

Yes indeed there is so big difference
between being submissive
and being just a beggar in love

This first is beautiful giving pleasure for two
The second one is just a lazy and tiring type
Nothing to offer just to take
Love is to offer yourself in the way you wish both
Beauty is love

Bondage

The more you bound my body the more you relieve my soul
every day I feel better with this
no chains, no fear
lives here
just
love
and
the wish to give you more

To men

Any man who didn't touch my heart
Those who didn't come closer for a bit
Doesn't take a part
In the mystery of my life
But each one of you
Who came here
For love
Is part of me now
Is the treasure I gain
Inside
All of you are great!
All of you are sweet
All of you know
What the beauty between you and me is
All of you are here
Forever
Even if all we had was just a while
You are still the best thing I have ever had a chance
To receive in this life

Just don't say

Just don't say that I don't love you enough
Just don't say that it's only you whose love is real
You don't even know how every touch
Comes deeply here to me
How this creates my every move, every day
If I'm not good enough so ok go away
And never come back again
You don't understand or it's not for you
This world I'm living for
It's not for you this heart
It's not for you
This light and smile
If it's giving you not this that you want
Be free to go or be free to love
Just don't say I don't love you enough
I am as I am
If you don't see beauty if you don't accept
Simply go away

This moment of light

It's such a sweet taste
Of this fresh unexpected feeling of light
That comes suddenly to you
From the sight of a beautiful stranger
Who touches your heart so merrily from the start
By look, by smile, by touch or some words
That flow gently to your soul and you know
It's something in the air again
It could be this man this special one for you
And you smile you don't know why
Just somehow
And mostly this is all you have
Just this moment in space to catch
To enjoy and to feel this something special in the air
This gentle breeze of life this little light
It can turn into many forms
Dance poetry or song
Sometimes it's a beginning of a relationship too
Sometimes even something more
You wish to believe that - in love
But only time will show this
If you want to know
Now the only thing you have is this smile
And some little need to do something more
And to go for it deeper a bit
We never know but this smile is all
We are looking for
And what we adore each time it comes to us
For good or for a while

It's not sex what is all about

In this what we do
It's not really sex that it's all about
Sometimes it's love yes
This something special in the air
That lets you sing all day
But mostly it's relationship we learn to build
To know each other more
To go one our journey through the world
To know ourselves and to share smiles and joy
That's all we are for.

Sex is good for a while
To know if we can go further a bit
Or if it is exciting
If we can create some pleasure
And dream, some trust between
And to go on without any fear
Into this lovely trip
Between you and me
That's all we long for.

How many lovers from the dream can you handle?
Who knows this?
I don't, I search
Even if I know I love
This hunger to know more
Put me into another dream
To live in
It's kind of madness maybe
But who cares about this?
If it brings nothing but smiles and tears
If it lets me see more clear
What this life is

Where is the end?
If I go to you
And stay for good
Will I close all other doors?
Or I'll cherish my dreams still
Who knows what the future brings?
Is any winner in this this story of life?
Is any up and down in it?

You know that I love you
But I know also this that love
Is the shortest from never ending things
This passion between you and me
Is all what we can really win

Let's go for it and don't think of the rest of the world
Don't care about any form
Just drink it
Until all is alive and full still

I know what art is
So don't say you will teach me this
I know this life a bit
Or I can imagine and dream it
I need my freedom to live and to be back to you
To be sure you are this man I long for

You are the man I wish to own and kiss
To be with
I'm just not sure if this life
Is not too short or not too long
For only one story of love.

Not nice guest

Being naughty
is just a little part of this
what the lovely man
should be for me
and you are not,
so if filling the hole
is all you are looking for,
well go on
but far from this home.

Playing

I'm as a child
Who is playing in this
Game of life
With a smile
Sometimes I cry too
When I lose
Something I love so much
But after a while
I smile again
When I see you came
To me
again
My gentle man.

It's better like this

So you went back to the mother of your child now
I know it's better like this for both
I know sometimes we have to leave
Sometimes we have to be a realist
But it's so sad we never met each other and now it is too late
You know my love, with the time
We just put on us higher luggage that's all,
All these loves that come, some stay, some go
It's all in us after years - some we left but some we can't
Sometimes we are even coming back to put it again on us
Depends what we need at times,
I don't know if it's bad or no
But recently I have very colourful life
I know you don't like it,
But actually we are not together
Maybe we never will,
Though I always feel you near,
You were this first sweet man
Who came here for love
And I gave you this from all my heart
But it's not easy to be in love just here i know
For you and for me too
I need all the time some touches, so I have them
I didn't know there are so many beautiful men on this world,
Yes I'm also a naughty one
And they give me smiles
And yes I do dance for them too
And they say to me the same sweet words as you
And they are beautiful in this
Maybe you stop loving me
Knowing what I do
I don't know you are easy to leave
And I can understand this I think.
Maybe it's all for some time of my life
So enjoyable I don't know
Maybe I have that kind of soul
The only thing I wish is that you will not forget me
And sometimes think of me with a smile in your heart,
You are still so special one for me
Though you were never treating me well I think
But even these few touches you gave me and smiles
Mean a lot and thank you one more time
To put so much love into my heart,
I'll always have and keeping you inside
Even if we really never met you will stay
Like that
As you are just so beautiful lover
I have ever had

So long lover

It's so long ago I haven't seen you
lover
is it all good in your life?
are your days full of smiles?
oh please let me know soon
I wish to know all you do
and if you are happy now or no
and if your face is so sweet
as it was before
and if your eyes
are hiding the same light and love?
oh comeback to just tell me this
please

Few words to lover

Wonderful lover of mine
are you busy today?
I miss your face and smiles so much
and I hope to see you soon,
you gave me so much pleasure
so much joy
just being with me the way I long
and this wondrous feeling of hope
for the new miracle of love
my lover my wonderful man
who I wish to meet soon and kiss and caress
and be with one day
Have a great night and day too and be back soon

Good time for good bye

Yes it was good time to say goodbye
I'm strong enough now to survive
I'm able to go further
and to appreciate all things that happened to us
you were such a lovely man
and it was a perfect romance
but it's time to go
our separate ways - I know
and I accept
so goodbye
for good
and have a beautiful life
my wonderful sweet one
love

Mistake

You just didn't understand
Any message I had to you
So now I know
What I'm standing on
I just lost another love of life
And even friend I had hope to have in you
And all illusions I have had so far too
Yes I see now very clear
Yes it was all just a big mistake
We did both
And yes all I see
Is that we are all alone on our way of life
And all lovers betray
That's how you have used to this and live again
And be born for another day for another dream
Of perfect love
That will come.

P.S. It's a kind of monster you had to see in me I think,to write to me such things so much
anger in this, my dear...
I'm sorry but I'm far away right now from all this
I'm so alone here and smiling still oh how all looks sometimes clear...
Such emptiness in such a great dream.

I run to you with open heart to crash suddenly into the wall.

Bitter-sweet

Oh yes you are not only sweet
But also very bitter one
How should I forget
And be silly enough to share with you my thoughts
You are the man who needs
Just another type of woman than I'm
I can't be true to you
It kills us and this love
This love which doesn't exist anymore
Or maybe it was all just imagination?
But no, too much anger in you
After my words
But you left me, do you remember?
You did
So what did you expect?
Sometimes we all have to fight
With this madness inside
I'm not without a fault
I know I can hurt
The same way you do
What is wrong with us, my love?
Where this path leads us?
Oh but actually all is gone
So what to worry about?
You can make me a fool
Or even the last idiot of this world
I can say many not important words
But at the end
All I can do
Is just to face this true
That you are this one I love
But it doesn't matter anymore
I lost you I know
I have to go my own wrong
Pointless way right now
Bye bye
Maybe you are right
Live your life
I hope I'll find some sense in mine
But you know that perhaps
It'd be a bitter moon
Between me and you
So maybe it's better like this

Good your answer is
so we can really go in peace right now
No one hurts anyone
All are winners
In this case
All stay tall no one fools anyone
It's just no way for us that's all
How easy is this right now
I can go with a smile
Thank you for this my love
You are one who is able to kill me by your words
You have to be careful too
Goodbye my love
Goodbye stay in peace forever

Forgive me

I didn't know I can be so cruel in love
So it all just hurts you that I'm here
That all makes you feel insane
Because you can't
Have me the way you wish
Only because you are weak enough
To not do it
Only because we live too far away...
Yes I'm a bit cruel I know
But sometimes you just run
And you don't think too much
What you do
You just run for this that you find beautiful
And I found you
I crash in to your life as a bomb
Now I see this
I didn't know it will be like this
Believe me
I didn't plan this
But now I see it's all my fault
Please forgive me
Forgive me
To make a hell in your soul
Forgive me
That you fell in love
Forgive me
That we can't be together for real
Forgive me
That I'm here still so smiling and tall as you say
Even if you tried so hard to trample me down
Just to forget me
Forgive me
That I was so blind, my love
Forgive me my write
Forgive me that I fell in you too
Forgive me
That I'm so far away from you
Forgive me to not be even faithful to you
Forgive me to let you down
Forgive me all my faults
I'm guilty it's not you
You are just beautiful
That's all

You were harsh to me
Just because you wish me to leave you in peace
I shall respect this and I will
Thank you to let me live still.

The theatre

Love turned into the form of art
This site is my private theatre
And my heart plays on this scene another act
It's real though it's still the play
But love you see is here
I wish you are the main watcher and actor as well
But I don't mind to be seen by all
When I sing my song filling the pages of my life's book
I never know who will come on the stage
To let me scream or dance more
Meantime there is a peace or little monologue
But this theater still lives here and welcomes all.

To a beautiful stranger:

This story of us was wonderful
And even the end of this
Is acceptable right now

It's just because we can't be together.

You said it's because
I'm too beautiful and I hurt you
You want me to leave you alone for good
You say that I'm a winner and you lose
But I see my self ugly right now
And I lost something so special
And I still can't come to terms with it
I don't even know when to leave.
What success did you mean telling me this actually?

And it's all just because we can't be together

Simple recipe to have a woman (at least her heart):

Attract her the way you are
Let her enter freely your life
Fall in love
Then leave her
With a bang
Then you have her
Forever perhaps
Just don't forget to let her know
That all you do
It's just because you love

Because as you know we appreciate these things
which we wanted and we lost
the most.

Goodbye my lover

You see it is much better like this
To leave this way without anger and regrets
You forget I'm a whiles collector
And I can't have bad memories
It's not a good way for me
Just to live with sadness and hate
You are still able to make me happy
or destroy me as well
So it's good that your mysterious plan fell
And we stay beautiful to each other
And we can stay in peace
Knowing only this that if we could
We will be together.

Yes the world is as big and beautiful
as your imagination that's true
So thank you too for being so beautiful
And filling my days with love, passion and joy
You were just as you should be, my love
To make me the woman I'm right now
I hope I was able to leave some little sign in your heart
And that whenever you will think of me
You will smile and just feel all right
That something like that
suddenly happened inside your heart
Never regret never be sad
It's best like this
We leave
But we still have our memories
We still have our dreams
And this life as no one else
Because we feel and we are real
That's all that matter
My dear lovely sweet lover man
Yes I can accept this goodbye
But I'll stay with my memories
This you can't take away from me
I do not agree :)

I love you too

I love you but you know and I too
That this is the light type of love
I don't see us as a husband and wife
I just smile when I see you are around
And all in you is so beautiful to me
And I love to stay near

Hunting

Once you asked what I mean by telling about this hunting here
But when I say this I don't mean anything wrong,
It's just I know you love to discover new wonders around
You search all the time and you gain new treasures on your site
You love to feed your soul like that and this is all right
But I see this just as a kind of hunting you need to live
Going to sleep with a new smile
And I know what you feel maybe because
I'm mostly there too just on the other side of this little dream
We own
If you want to know
I love this hunger in you and this need too
To discover new things around
You are a type of charming guy
And I love to be your friend.

Yes I know we said good bye to each other but

Yes we said goodbye
Yes I know
I'm impossible
Yes I know
I wrote too much
Yes I know I touched you
Not even once
Yes I know
That all I do is the cause of mess
Between me and you
But baby
I don't wanna lose you
If you love me still please
Don't go
Stay
Inside my world
Be here still
You know we can live
Just like this
I understand the troubles with moving
To me or to you
But all I feel is just an emptiness now
When I think you have gone
If you really have to go it's ok
But don't do it only because I did this or that
It doesn't matter at all
I love you
You should know
If it was only because some of my words
Please come back
I love you
And I care
I never want to hurt you again
I never want to let you feel blue
I promise to be good.
Don't go
Please stay
I need you more than air

You back my love

Love is the way
You and me
Feel each other here
Love is touch
Of your words
So sweet for me
Love is faith
In you and me
Let's be together like this
My love be here for me
As I'll be
And smile to me
That's all I need
My sweet
That's all I need

Being one

You make me wanting to be
This one special girl
You can see like this
You dream of, my sweet
How I wish to be
This one you are looking for
This one so gorgeous, so sexy
And so warm
Who is burning under the first touch of your glance
On her always naked body for you
Waiting to be seen, to be touched more
By your lovely flying soul
That let her feel so good

Just as I feel right now watching
Your charming dreams here
My dear

Down to Earth

And again
All I can do my man
Is just to dream
Of our sweet love
We have here
In our lovely trip
Through you and me

And all I wish
Is just that you could
Take a pleasure from me
So in love with you
Still

Oh, down to earth
It's so hard to be
When you are near.

All because of you

It's all because of you, my darling
If my life seems to be a wonderful one
It's just because I found you
If my words can touch you and give you warmth
It's because you lighted me for you
If I'm special for you I feel this way too
And I smile but I'd never be like this if not you,
My love
I'm alive because of you
Because of this that I feel for you
And because of this open book
I write still and I wish, I wish so much to be here
I don't know when and how we meet
One day but, me too, my love
I wish this so much and I live for this right now
Just as for another smile from your side

Your poetry

Your poetry
Talks to my senses
Your visions have so much
Lovely tasting smells of life inside
Your love is
Full of charming things
I could not see here
If not you and your words
So sweet to me
Which get on my senses
As nothing else
I love when you talk to me
Like this
I love the light you bring to my life
I love this desire I have
From the time I saw you
First time
And I love to live
With the sight of you
Inside.

So natural

So naturally it comes to me
The way you touch
My dreams
The way you create me
As a girl
So wanting you still

Fragile line between us

My love
I wish to be only
A reason to smile for you
But sometimes
I'm afraid that
Whatever I say or I do
Is touching you
Not the way I wish to
So tender is this
Little commitment
So fragile
I have to be careful more
For this what I say
Each word, each action
Can be too much to stand
Can let you feel down
And this is the last thing I want

Feeling you

I always know
When you are on the other side
I just come on this site
Always in the right time
We almost don't speak on line
Maybe it's just too hard
We are too much in love
So it's better just like this
Yes messages are nicer for now
More safe
To not crash anything
We have.

You came then
Oh you know
How much you get on me still
But at the same time it's so easy
To destroy this
But yes I love
You still
Yes, yes
We are as one
My love, my man
Nothing has change
Come to me again
One day
I long for it
Always
And I live
For this.

Little fears of the heart

Suddenly such sadness
Flowed in to my heart
You seem to be so far away
My love my beautiful man
And I'm in the middle of this colorful crowd
Just to feel how empty is my heart right now
When I'm not sure if all I do is not
Just one step to lose you on my route
I love you
Please don't forget
I love you
And I'm just lost
Because I simply don't know what to do
To have you a bit closer to me right now
Why I must miss you so much?
Why do I waste so much time for
All around?
I'm just lost without you
And I can't stand this silence
I need breathe by love, I need
To prove my self every day
That you are this man
You are this one
I'll never ever wish to lose
I'll never ever stop to love
Even if it hurts me sometimes
When I'm not sure
If it's not too much for you
This me all
I'm so afraid you just want to go
Because you can't see here beauty
Or because it's tiring this love
Or because you don't believe anymore

Just one your word is enough

Just one your word, my love and all sadness disappeared
You are the most wonderful man of this world
And I'm the most happy and lucky girl
To have your heart and soul
I know

It's just

It's just that you fill my days by something
I can't live without any more
The most important little thing
that let all system in my mind and soul work
Without this I can't handle my days
I can't feel safe
I can't enjoy all what this life brings to me
and feel happy and feel free
to go one this journey and to love
Maybe it's because…
when you once taste
this special charm of real love
anything else is not so good for you anymore
to enjoy and to go for
Maybe I could find
a bit similar atmosphere
to create this special warm in my heart,
this belief, this charm but no it's never the same
I've found you and from now
it's just so important to me
that without it
I don't feel me enough to ever move out
to live without you inside,
so I will
But oh how happy I'm to see you again so close to me
My dear, my sweet, wonderful one
Oh yes also bad sometimes but so full of charm
In each thing you say, or you do,
you are just so beautiful
Such magic I can't resist at all
So there is no more to do but enjoy and take it all
I live by this what you offer to me
To create more love, to make you warm enough
And to make you as happy as I'm right now
With you, my love.

Waves

Our love
Is as the wave
from one to another promise
I fly high to fall down
Into disappointment
but after years
I used to us like this
and I never lose my faith
That one day
We really meet
My man

And this Faith
is all my religion now
From the time
I saw you and I fell
For the miracle
Which filled me
So merrily

Winter time

The winter time is coming soon
Between me and you
Now all we know
Is that you are not going to come
At all
So now it's a silence time
To forget the sadness that came suddenly
To smile again one day
Perhaps to believe
From the start like nothing happened
Like you really wish to come here
Like you really love and wish to be still
And for good
Forever mine
It's such a sweet dream we have
So it's not easy to leave it and go
To all these real things around
That are and will be still
For real
But you and me
Have to be silent now
To forget again
This little disappointment
This little shame
That here is just a play
But no one should know this
Yes we have to believe still
To have this
My dear
It's such a lovely thing
So special dream

What should I do?

Your love is
Just an answer of my needs
You are coming each time
I'm calling you and I wish
You to be here
When I crave for you
Using the right words
But you are never here
When I'm silent
When I'm like this
You simply disappear
How it can be?
What should I do to make you
More active
More real?

The puppet

Yes that's it
You are here
When I set the strings
In motion
When I'm not doing it
You simply disappear
You exist on my request
In the world of my dreams
You are here
When I give you the sign
When I make you alive
By writing this story
On and on
I need to write
To have you inside
And to live
In my own theatre
In my own beautiful dream
Which became the part
Of mine and yours existence
As more I'm afraid
You could disappear
As more deeply you can live here
What if I close this book?
Will you go away
Without any word?

Yes I love you still

After a few days of my silence
You doubt and ask me if I love you still?
My darling
You don't know how much it cost to be quiet to you
For a while
You don't know why?
I did this little break?
I just wished to give you a little time
To miss me
As you do right now
I was just afraid for a moment too
That you don't need me so much
As I need you
That's what this little silence was for
But you know
How much I miss you here
How much I need to be sure
Of your heart all the time
To live, to go on this beautiful life's trip
Yes I love you my darling still
And I'm so happy you miss me a bit

Just keep the touch

I wish to be close enough
To hear your thoughts
But you are far now
and a bit silent sometimes
I can't feel you inside
This makes me lost
And I need to call
I need to ask
For this little you
Inside my soul
I need your thoughts so much
Please keep the touch
and love, yes love me
this is all I need
To live
To smile
when I open my eyes
waking up
to another day
with you here
I live to be yours
Don't you know
I live waiting
For another touch
From you
As it was
before.

Little marks

Soon the last mark on my skin
Will disappear
It will be hard to believe
All it was real
Perhaps it was just a sweet dream
We both have had suddenly
Perhaps it wasn't your lips
Touching me
Not your palms not your ...
Are you real, are you real and mine?
Or I was dreaming?
Should I forget all this here?
Do you want me to stay silent
And calm dreaming still
Just smiling from time to time
That perhaps one day
Such dream can open me again
To go for, to wish, to feel you
Just as it was a moment ago?
So.. You have been inside me and where are you now, my darling?
Around still?
With me?
Near?

Our sweet sin

It's a privilege
To stay
Your whore
I've never felt so good
Before

Licking
Smacking
Sucking
Oh, so sweet
Is our little sin

We grow up
Together in it
In to the new beginning
In to the life

We are
As we are
Poets
Lovers
Sinners
That's all because
You are so beautiful you
And you let me be
Your whore

You have a gift
To change the meanings
Of the words
My baby
My love
How it's sweet
Your cock
In my mouth
Let's start again
I wish to have you
In my hand now

We were there
In our small room
And we did
As we want
Yet still
So little me
You let me to show

To you
No time, no place
To use all charms
We have to meet again
But I'm afraid
We wont have the time to lose again
And I'll need just to taste you, feel you
Listen
And to be your girl
again

It's just suddenly I felt
Unsure a bit
Am I great enough
To be your love
This lady you need
Your queen
I can be your whore
Yes, this I can

I hope you were satisfied of me this way
Did my mouth work well for your pleasure,
Or should I learn more?
Tell me
I need to be your perfect whore
I need to give you the best love
I wish this and I want to know
How to give you more
And more

I forget to show you
My dance
We have to start again
This romance
You have to see me
Dancing for you
It's the part of the secret ritual
You have to see
I'm princess too
For you

But to be your whore
Was so good
You know
And I wish to be like this
Again
Yes, my man

I love to finger my self
Thinking that it's you
Doing it so sweetly
Still
I love you
Doing it
To me
Here
And in all of those places
Train
Cinema
Such a wonderful things
We create
Being together
I miss
Your smile
The way you move
Our steps
Harmoniously connected
Your arms on my waist
Holding me tight
Your hands in mine
Our kisses in the crowd
On a bus on a tube
And your face
Your eyes watching me now
My beautiful
Oh, how beautiful
You are.

I can't give you this feeling of loss

I never gave you any chance
To feel real loss of me
You do not know then
How violently but merrily you could
Keeping me inside
After my depart
I'm not strong enough
To give you this
I've never been strong enough
To leave
As you did to me
Twice
Perhaps
I'd never know
How much I love you
And have you
If you never tried
To tear us apart
For a while.

I should let you know
All colours of love
But I'm not able
To do that at all.

But you too
Never do this to me again
It's too sad
We live too far for this
To hurt each other this way
We have our own distance love
For years for now
And this is enough
To miss and to live

And to keep it within
As a treasue and our own dream
Don't you think?

So beautiful words still

Oh so beautiful are your words to me
Again still
I hope you are not telling me this
just to fuck me one more time
But you know you can do it any way
So it's sweet from you
To be always so nice
Any way
That's why I love you so much

Anarchy

How it is
That this little anarchy in love
Makes me so happy
I just worry a bit
How are you with this me
So open
Suddenly
Here

Discovering

With you
I feel like
I just discovered
How beautiful love and sex
Can be
With all this
What is
In this short space
Between my and your lips

or

other things

we use

to this

I'm sorry but I love it

Why each time I put another poem
On this wall
I feel like I lost a bit of us
This what we have
I feel I can lose you
But it doesn't stop me at all
I love this risque
I love to wait
Your answer
What you can tell after all
I need your reactions
Like fresh water to drink
I can't live by memories just
Or dreams
I need you now
Even angry sometimes
Even mad
Even surprised unsure
But you
In love
Forgiving
Or amazed
I need you near
I'm sorry to be
Such a little girl
Using tools I shouldn't maybe
Writing about you and me here
I'm sorry
But I love it

Playing with you

What a strange game
You wish to play in
My poet friend
Don't you know me yet?
You search the answer
Which is so easy to find
Who is Ania?
You ask
She is nothing more but woman in love
Sometimes an angel sometimes a whore
Whatever name you can find for her
It's just a word
To find out
What the woman can see
Going deeper inside her own dream
But this dream seems to be so real recently
So she is enjoying it
And dancing still
Just when the music plays
It's fairy dance
Inside her

My song is to him

Is this song right
For your ear?
Your words tickled me
Sweetly this morning
So familiar they are
Oh, but you know
That my dance is free
And my heart is singing
To my lover's ear
He is my dream still
And his voice is the one
I can hear among a million suns
And it lets me feel the universe
And a million stars
That let my soul dance
What game
Could be better than this?
What I can hear
In a voice from my lover's dreams?

I love when you are good to me

I love the way you let me know
That you don't mind and that you love me what ever I do
And I won't lose you so easily as I'm always afraid that I could
You don't even know how much I love when you talk to me
How much I love that you are here still
I love when you are good and sweet
I love that you let me feel so good each time you come
However I'm able to express it to you
It's real and it's wonderful
My heart is yours
And this makes me feel
As never before
I learn each day to love you more
This is what I was born for

The scent

I wonder where
Do you feel the scent of me now
And how intense it is still in your mind
Can you see me still, can you find
In all of those places you were writing about?
Do you remember I asked you once
"Steal me"
You said that you already did
Really?
Wasn't just a loan?
I could think like this
When I don't see you now
Only your last words "don't worry"
Let me believe and let me be calm
I wish it could be forever.

We know the taste of paradise now

Picture of heaven
We created once
And we even touched this
Even tried
All of those tasty colours and smacks
All of those branches and fruits
We know, we tasted
Oh just why
I feel so moved
Watching some silly sexy film
On one of those sites
And why I'm so sad
All this is so far away right now?
But you love you said
And you think every day
Of our time together
I have to wait than
I know
It's just so hard sometimes
When there is no you around
Not even word
Any touch
Just memory and promise
But I know you are here
Inside me still
And in all
Of those sites places some faces too
And our words here
And our souls
I feel so rich now
Though still hungry too
How amazing is this all
With you right now.

What to worry about?

What do I have to do
Just to be happy that's all
Each day is coming bright
With love living inside my heart
So what to worry about?
Oh maybe just that he should't work so hard
All the time
Maybe that I could work more
A bit right now
Oh actually I think
There is nothing still
All are fine
We spend another day of life
With a smile and this is great
Why childish you think am I?
I don't understand
What kind of problems I can have
With this?
Who can't understand?
All are good and nice to me
So why worry?

Yes I do worry a bit
That maybe you work too much recently
But from other hand I know
It's your entire world right now
It gives you power to live and to smile
And to make this world
A bit more tasteful and special place to live in
To enjoy
So actually
I love you are like this
So multi skilled, so active
I wish I could be like you too
I adore this and I'm proud of you
Except the fact you are so sweet and cute
Also that you know when to say no
And how beautifully you can make love
And talk
And you say you love me
And this make me feel so good
And then I know that this life is just so beautiful.

Sweet buster

I love in you even this
How sweet buster you are
Telling me that your heart was with the Polish team
But money you gave for another one
Which you find better in your mind
What a clever bad boy you are !
I adore it
It makes me smile
Can't help
You are just wonderful
Perfect
Cute
Sorry to say so
But I can't stop my words
After your phone call
I'm too happy to stop my self
I couldn't even sleep last night quite long
I had so many lovely emotions in me
I was just so happy
Amazing

You are welcome

I feel good when you find your self comfortable
Within my soul
You know you are welcome
I feel good in the place you create too
All your pictures are so captivating so intriguing
And make me wish more
Please don't stop
You let my mind and heart grow
With wishes of talk
And this is actually all that I enjoy
Right now

Dream but real

Even if all we have here is nothing but a wonderful dream
I'm able to die for it
Or at least fulfill my days with joys and little tears
And thoughts so magical and sweet
That let my days come with new dreams
Which make my life so special trip

For all this I can only thank you
And my own heart so full of love
I suppose
And few beautiful friends too
Yes, for sure.

Hungry poet

So hungry you are now
It seems like a picture
Of a man sitting on the branch
Who is watching
His muse
And all scaps of her juicy cunt
Which is giving new light
To fulfill his mind
For more
Poetry
Is this good relationship
To go on?
This little exchange of two mad minds
Dancing on the wall
Of our dreamlands?

The train

I had little dream
About the train yes
Wasn't Orient Express?
And the stranger on the way
Whose glance makes me feel
So naturally naked
Again?
And the journey was long
Very deep
Surprising
Sweet...
Yes
I love trains too
I think so…

Tension

All is fine
Yes
Just why each time
It hurts the same
This lack of answer
This silence
I should used to this
I know
I should be calm
Happy
And I am
Just this silence
For a moment
Is so heavy still
I can't stand this
But don't want pressure you too much
Do not want expect
You are perfect
I know this
So all what I can do
Is just to believe
I know
It's just sometimes
When I don't know what to do
To let you be close enough
To listen your thoughts
To hold

Be positive
Yes I know
It's all within my mind
It's not your fault
I'm just too crazy now
I should fight
With such a tension inside
With such thoughts
It's an obsession
Not a love
But I love you
Yes I do
I feel you in each little cell of me
You live inside here
So why all these worries about?
I'm silly I know
Just be back soon
My love.

So easy

Oh, so good
You came back
I can rest a bit
I can smile
So happy I'm right now
It's so easy you see
Happy with you
Sad without
Nothing between
Nothing around
Just me and you
Inside each other
Is all the world
Is love

Whatever

Our love
Is such a beautiful long story
Each single word has a meaning in it
Each thought
We care so much to not spoil
This what we have
At the same time
We are just as we are
Free inside, so natural
In each action we do
And something else too
This that is the most wonderful
Whatever comes to our minds
Whatever we decide to do
It's always just so beautiful
And exciting too
It's because of this natural charm of yours
I suppose :)

Life with you

Life seems so exciting
When you have your lover beside still

Yes

Even this simple yes is more than enough to make my heart aroused

Our picnic

Inside my head
Is nice for you
Oh it must be
Because all of those thoughts
That came to my mind
From the time
You live here
So sexy thoughts
I can say
So fine

It seems you talk during it
Me after this
Yet our minds compare
As all other parts of us
Fit to each other
To live together
In the stars
Yet still
Down to Earth
We are
Romantic but real.

Missed conversation

When I'm with you I wish nothing but make love
After some time I love to write but when is this little spark
For an interesting conversation between us?
I'm afraid it's not possible to do that
Not important so much
As long as you find my mind attractive place
For you
To stay
For good

Into the shadow

My silly greed for daily emotions
Kills another day
Of light
And turn my mind into abandon
So many words messing the air
I sent to you again
What is it for?
If nothing but you
I wish to have in my world
But I play still
Each time when new refreshing smiles
These little sparks of mystery
Put the shadow between you and me
And turn my world of words
In to the cloud of your silent voice
Please stop
I wish so
You know that the best feeling I keep inside
Is this one from you
Nothing can change this
Only you
Or this mess I make around

Don't say I won't find my home

What I can do with my wishing silly mind
Where to go with it
If I search nothing but love
But each time I'm closer to it
It seems I'm not able to drown deep

Is it something wrong with me?
What is this practical love you talk about
You don't believe I'm able to love like this?
You think I'm always far away from these who I should be with?
There is no help for me?

Please do not say this
I wish to hide right now right here
Not wandering anymore
There is no need
I know my heart and its greed
Don't say I want more than I should
Don't say I will never be able to find home

I'm a bit away now I know
My mind flies to another land
But do you think so
It will be always like this?
No I hope you are wrong

It was just another step to do
And right now there is another one
Finally I'll rest in his arms for good
Don't say I wont
You don't know this at all
Please don't say such words

I was never more sure anything but this
That one day I'll have to leave.

Should protect you

All I have to do is just to learn
How to take you away
From all these dark clouds that suddenly come
I should protect this little castle of us
From the war
Hiding you in to the warm shelter
Of silent night
We have to wait in calm and peace
For another day with the sun
These storms are not good for you
I should remember and erase this all
I should protect the peace inside your soul
No need to rush it no need to say any word
That could just let you worry again
Yes there is always a smile after rain
So why share this all
There is no point
The war is over now
And we are born again
To another day
And a walk hand in hand

How much me you need?

Just sometimes
I worry a bit
You don't really need daily me
You have your world, pleasures, thoughts
That are so completely unknown
To my world
No me there still
It's ok I love when you come back
So suddenly sweet guest you are
Each time
So good to see you again
Yet still
I worry a bit
No daily me you need

Trapped in delight

I'm here
Trapped
In this warming cave of my mind
Demanding fresh juices
To fly
You have touching spirit
I love it
So live here
This light is my daily food
From now
So I devour you
And live still
The pleasure of it
Is too big
To stop
I think

Addictive world

Higher knight
Jump to this little star
That I'm keeping hanged above
Just for pleasure for both
What can be wrong in it?
Addictive you said
So what?
Can you find something around
Better
Right now?
This outside world
Is nothing so special
We all know it
So better drown
Deeper here
So you can eat
All sweets of my spreading wings
Created for you and me
To love and live
Beautifully
From one to another day
We can fly like this
There is nothing else
Worth a while
More
Than this little spark of delight
In your mind

By the way

Who is more addictive type
me or you?
Is this a competition we do?
What are you planning now?
Day two?
or the end of us both?

Labyrinth

Another empty corner
Trapped me here
Yes it was a nice ride today
My little wildly need
Was dancing freely
For your eyes
Such art for art
Smiling gates
The show for two
But in fact
It was nothing so special
Yes nice little ride
To the stars
We all love it
From time to time
Just run rabbit run
But you know
And me too
There is an empty corner
And not enough
To fill your mind and soul
With real joy and something more
Than simple pleasure
Which is easy to find
But this is not what we really care about
Yet still nice

Muse

I know that my poetry
Makes you hard
Is this bad?

ALL YOUR LETTERS

I love these capital letters you use
Writing to me your words
I love the message you include in them
I love each single thought
I can look at it and feel it so well
Sometimes they are as a flowers
Touching deeply my senses by its natural beauty
Sometimes they are as a tender through strict little pins
That let me aware of my actions just done before your eyes
I love all tastes of them
And I wish doing more
To receive all kinds of words you give
As a proof of your love or your warning as well
All kinds are always so special and right
And hits home as you say so
I love them as you I love

Somebody else is the lover

Maybe this can make you silent now
And I know it'd be lost
Not only for me but to the world
But this cunt
Which you crave for
Is closed

It's nothing but mind

What makes you feel so fine
Seeing nothing but this naked mind?
This little spark of naughty smiles
Don't let you sleep at night?
Ha ha
Oops I shouldn't laugh this way
I know exactly how it works for me
And how dangerous it is
This mind creation in your head
Is all what really makes you mad
But happy too
So why not?

Library

She belongs to another race
Knowledge hunter
She follows good names
To use them
For her own progress

In mean time
We are here
Drinking
The wisdom
Of our shelves
Unwritten still
Books of emotions

The warrior

You are a big city warrior
And me just a water nymph
From one of these pretty looking lakes
You wish to go by one day
But you don't have the time enough
Busy in your big hard beautiful world
I'm waiting here still
Smiling because I know
That in fact you are here
Inside drowned quite deeply
Just as it should be
With me

When you say "I miss you"

When you say
I miss you
I just wish to get hold of your beautiful head
Put it tight to my breast
Kissing you on your sweet cheek
And kissing more
Your lips
Your eyes
Your ears
And go down too a bit
Just to see this wonderful rush desire in your glance
With such a great passion and love within
And all your trills and words
To feel and hear
I wish

Two birds

There is a beauty
In your words
That I can't deny
There is a spirit I love to drink
Day and night
There is a mystery I wish to follow too
And there is a story we create both
So merrily
Floating here
Among the pages of our own
Realities
We live
We are nothing but birds
Searching wild but cosy nests
Among the trees
Of our dreams
Smiling

Journey to heaven and hell

Been traveling two days
Little journey to the dark side
Seems fine
For a while
Discovering new
Exciting pictures
From little hell
For sell
Oh, sweet sin
Seems to be
For a moment
Until you see
Something too dark
And all fun is gone
Only scar
Is it all real?
Too horrible,
Disgusting
So easy to find here to follow to have
Hell for sell
On the Earth
No boundaries
No heart
Just a big fat cock to smack
Right know bitch!
Slut!
Go one
Yes do your job!
Fuck, fuck
Deeper whore
Yes Master!
Yes!
Sir please more
Hit me fuck me
Piss
On me
Can't stand this anymore
It's too much
She can't
Like this
They are monsters
Nothing more
Pigs, jerks oh
No human at all
It was nice fun at the start yes
I can't deny
Some play
Some smile

And pleasure and pain
Yes
The theater
But then one picture too much
And I wish to run
Just run
And forget this hell
She can't love this
I don't believe
It was rape nothing more
Disgusting scaring sick
What a gate I opened suddenly and why
To be aware to know more?
I don't really know
What is inside human race
Darkness
Madness
Is there god behind?
Can he save all of them?
Can he cure mad minds
We all can have
And give them the rain
And heaven
Without pain
Give them forgiveness or dream
Not boring but beautiful
Acceptable, a bit wild, free
Still black and white
Still full of excitement and this joy of fight
But clear, more clear
Not like that
Please
Please god if you exist
Don't let me see such movies!
It's too far from love and beauty
It's too far from reality
And dream I have to live
It was hard trip
Too much to stand too much to understand
I can't get it
Yes into the shadow
I can find
This deep extreme joy
Of submission
To explore
To feel to know
Yes it's still so many ways
To try to go
Until you see
Something what is just too much

And you know
You have to be back
To normality
What ever you think of this
Be back to your own sweet dream
Of love of heaven
Of you and me
Yes baby
I'm back
Nothing compares to us
And this love we have

Instead of all

Instead of all I loved when you say
That you respect my pussy
So you can't just come and go
And you will fuck it one hour or more
That was cute
Just as your cock
So different you are
From all
Even this wild part of you
Is just exciting and so good
This bad boy in you
Is wonderful
My sweet tender brutal you are
And this way it's a real pleasure
To be your whore
Yes, my love
You have a key to this door
Fits perfectly

Welcome

The sweetest things

It's so good to be back to you
And to know what is the sweetest thing
For me
It's your smile
I think
Yes I'm sure
And your voice of course
And your arm holding me tight
Yes all these sweet simple things
Are the best I think
And walk and laugh
from all these funny thoughts and words
That comes to mind
When we just spend the time
Together
Hand in hand
And this smile,
Yes this smile of yours
And your touch.

The melody of your words

Once again your words
Seem to be
As a melody flowing straight in to my heart
The sweetest one I could ever hear and have
So I sing this song all day
And all I want now is to dance
As you play
As you say
As you wish
My man, my dream
You are everything
And you cherish this
As me
It is all I was waiting for
You are right
My love

Listen your self

There are few who know
This one of possible truths
That perhaps there is not god above
And we are all alone
On this world
But don't listen to them
Only you know
If he is alive or not
Listen all voices that let you go deeper
Into your self
And listen to your heart
Then the way you go would be right
Even if you try to run away
All you believe in is yours
Just as a dream
Just as love

Any words

Any song in me today
Any dance, wish or play
Any word
Just this silent lack of you
Inside
Just this
I MISS YOU
I find

Silent

But after all
I'm happy to know
That I have a man
To whom I can tell
These words
Directly
And to feel
Even this
Silent answer in me
He is there
He needs
And he feels
The same
Just sometimes
Has no words as well
To tell how much
He misses me
So he is silent
Even more than me

Who is the winner

What if love is nothing but a nice song?
A poem, a wish, a joke?
A dream for those who are tired
To hunt more
Or too silly naive maybe one
For those who are weak too
For one who is not able to do anything more?
For these who need challenge
And fun
Is sex for some time
Perhaps
What is better than?
Depends
I suppose
It's good to try all
To know
There is no one way for all
Maybe even few ways in different time
We should try
Who is winner who lose?
In this game?
Who is more happy?
I don't know

You by my side

I was just lost for a moment in space
My dearest one
It's always this way when there is no sign
From you for a while
But I know all right now
And what is love
And what I want
This what I feel
When you come here
And you know so well
What I need
Is my entire world
Is love
And you by my side
Forever

I miss you

I miss you
Each time you are silent for few days
What to do with my self
Yes some messages around me all the time
Yes some smiles poems comments
Yes all the world around
I still have
But when you are silent
For a few days
I'm so terribly heavy
And I can't think of anything else but this
That you are silent
Any message today again
I just wait to smile
I'm so addicted to your thoughts in me
I shouldn't maybe
Have to fight with this
Have to live
As before
Yes I know
But I miss you
I dream of you
Each night
I have you inside all the time
Can't wait to touch you again
And it's a madness I know
This love shouldn't be like this
I should breathe
Just simply doing my things
And waiting for new
Sweet dreams you bring
With you smile,
With your words,
With your spirit
With your love
I know
But I miss you!
And only this
I can feel
Still
When you are silent
So completely
Just few words I need
To breathe to live
You know this
Come back
To me
My darling

Two persons

It's like two persons
Living together
One is still smiling cherishing this world
Dancing freely among the spaces of colourful dreams
Searching joys, new wishes, new things to play with, to keep
And this second one
So full of uncertainty
Weak emotions hidden a bit
So easy to go down with them
And forget
Your name and all meanings
So easy to destroy
The mood of glory and smile
How is that?

The parts of yours, which I love the most

I love your tongue and fingers the most I think
Oh and your voice
When you are saying all these sweet sexy things to me
Yes I love it
Of course I love your cock too
It's a really cute one
It's just that your tongue and fingers
Oh and this gorgeous voice of yours
Were first

So I love them
The most I think

Though yes it's hard to choose
What part of you is the sweetest one
I know
But this tongue penetrating me oh
And these fingers of yours
And the way you play with me by them
Oh and then all that you say
And your look
God how I miss this all
Right now...

Old description

So you were not disappointed, my darling
This warm gorgeous sexy imaginative one
With the wonder of life and lust burning in her eyes
Lying curled next to you
So suddenly
Yes this one you were dreaming about
On one of your sites
Is me..
It's still so sweet
To believe
To have you like this
To keep
All memories
All dreams
You don't even know how precious you are for me
And this wonder of life and all smiles
I feel just because you are here
In my mind, my heart, my life
It's you who has burned this light
And all I try from now
Is to keep this still
Is to believe
In us
for real

Can't help

You are so good in this art of seduction
That's why I love you so much too
You were born to be my love
And to make me the most happy girl
Of this world
You know?
Such a sexy guy as you
Makes me feel just wonderful
I can't help this
Why so?

I just want to sing this song for you
And follow you whenever you say I should go
And do whatever you ask for
That's why I was also born to, my love

Dreams too simple a bit

I met the man recently who said to me
That my dream is very simple one
Yes I think it is
But why to complicate things?
Is it not better to keep free space
Between me and you
For more art and love?
And what to wish more
If we have each other?
And we learn each day
How to make this simple case
More beautiful and real?
What more to dream about
Should I
And why?

It's all art in it

It's all art to keep things simple
Because there sre so many distractions around
So many sweet ways to taste, to try
So at times it's hard to be clear
Even with your self
And with all this that you need and want
Especially in this feelings world
You keep inside and you enjoy
As nothing else I suppose.

Holidays thoughts

I became calm
Drowned in thoughts of you
Just waiting when you will open your mobile phone
To hear the sound of the report
That you received the message
I sent some time ago
But it is still closed
No answer, so I wait
Another special book in the meantime
A Chinese author sweet sensitive girl
"Shanghai baby"
I could be as she is
I think
Only attraction this year is the sea
With waves here
Even my fisherman and his boat disappeared
But it's better like this
From the time you live here
And thoughts of you are all
I can drown in
And you are so mine
Inside and on the other side
Of my mobile phone
Right now
All seems similar each year
Though different still
My thoughts of you
Are deeper and with more certainty
That you are mine
Even living still
That far
You said to me once that your only dream is to be inside me
And what about now?
What are other dreams that you have?
If you already had me just as you dreamt of ?
So nice you said that you long for me even more now
That's what I feel and want too
My lover, my wonderful one
I'm so happy to have you
I can live without any people around me
But I like to keep a few friends in net
Can you understand?
Aspirations
As many of us
I wish to write a book sometimes
Have money to survive
And to keep this love I have now
Alive

Maybe move to London one day
I like this city the most I think
With its colourful happy crowd in a Piccadilly Circus at night
With all its calm lovely green parks
With all these monuments of ancient glory too
With the beauty of all the world
Living there
With its mess
I'm just afraid a bit
If I can find something to do there
Something not too hard
You know I'm not that strong
And full of enthusiasm for such things
To have all on my head
It's too heavy a bit
But always I can try, I think.

Messy Mind

It seems that you have a gift
To find for your self
A problematic girl a bit
Each monologue I have to you
It always sticks to the same point
I'm afraid that I'm not this girl
You can really love
Even if I wish this so much
Even when you say
From time to time
That you do
I need to keep it alive
All the time
Each day again from the start
I need to know this
And let you know too
That I just think of you
But at the same time doing it
I'm afraid so much
That I'm losing you
By my silly talk
How it's difficult
Just to keep silence a bit
Or saying few words
Just to let you know
That I'm here and I love
As you do this
From time to time
Until you are losing patience a bit
And keep silence
You busy responsible full of life man
And me who is doing nothing special still
And who so evidently needs your company each day
When perhaps I should keep my self as busy as you
Or at least pretend that I do
So many things as you
I keep my mind busy just
And sometimes can't keep my hands
Far enough from my mobile phone
Or messenger to not share some of this
What is running here
Just why I'm afraid so much
I can lose you
And can't stop writing
All weaknesses of my heart
Which gives you nothing except a feeling
That I'm not that strong as I should be
And maybe I even let you be confused a bit

It's terrible this need in me
And all this uncertainty
How you can stand this my love
How can I have so many silly problems
On and one childish impossible
God what a funny person human being is
Especially me right here
And all these crazy ideas
I know they are mad a bit
And selfish I'm in this
Can you love me
As I am right now?
Can you understand why
I need this so much?
And even if all seems
Funny and sad and piteous too
It's all me for you
And it's all I enjoy
Inside my heart
After all I'm not sure
If it won't be better to stay as we are
I just have to write less
To give you a chance
To miss me a bit
As well my mysterious personality
Because showing you all me
Can be killing
To this love and me
Maybe it's time
To leave my self
To start create something else
New perspective perhaps?
But all I have in me

Is you

What do I know of you then?
You are so sexy man
With this you say
The way you see things in life
Sometimes you are cruel a bit
With your opinions yes
About these who don't know
All this you do so well
These who have too easy life
You don't trust
Sometimes I'm a bit scared when you say so
If my life is enough difficult
To be the person you can adore

For something more that a pretty face or legs
It's just because I need so much your love
Yet still so beautiful you are in all this
That you think
God what to do to be sexy for you
Enough again
I said so many things you could call
Not fruitful and childish too
That you can't find any interest to continue
Why am I so silly with you
But at least so happy
When I get this little answer
For all this I say
Even when a bit hard you are
I feel nothing but love
And I'm all in smiles
Feeling your thoughts again
In me
I can enjoy them again and explore each colour of them in me
Until another wave of uncertainty flows through my mind
And I worry again to come back
To the same point, in me
Hopeless girl
Even being a bit cruel yet still beautiful you are to me
And I can't stop telling you this
Such a flatterer I became here
But it's only to you I'm like this
I can't stop my self and you know it's what I think
Even if it can be just funny to you at least.

What ever you plan to do after this
Just fuck me one more time please.

You didn't tell me
That you love me yesterday
I know it was all not necessary
This talk of rich and poor
Or other conditions
Or work
And compare this that you said
And what is true
To my self
But I'm a bit silly this way
I always take all to my self
Then all these thoughts you know so well
Flowing again through me
And all I wish is that you could say
Something nice

But at times you just turn in to silence
I can't change this
So have to calm down
And grow up I think
And have hope
That you love me
And such things can't change this
Even when I do not agree
With all that you say
I love when you do so
I love to hear your voice
It's always so cute somehow
This charm is in each step you do
Each word and the way you see this world
And your point of view for all these rich politicians too
Even when you are so cruel to them
And I think it's not all so bad as you say
I love when you do so
And at least I have to agree
You are right with most of this
What you believe in.
Oh actually I think
I'm totally simple one girl
And I always had
These problems you mention about
The low income
The only difference
Is this that I never tried
Real hard work
I choose another way to go
That's all
He has your profile

What amazing touch
Can't stop looking at this man
But not, now I see his face
Is not so sweet as yours
Not this glance not this charm
But profile
Yes it is similar and this smile
God, this smile
I can see your face
So well now
You are so clear in my mind
So sweet beautiful
What a wonderful feeling is this
Memory to keep
And you are mine still
As you say to me

I should never doubt in this
Amazing looking at his nose and the same cute line of his mouth
That remind me you give me so much pleasure
So suddenly incredible
Pleasure on the beach
I can say

Do whatever you want
Keep your world as far from mine as you wish
Just don't stop to love me please.

Our worlds are so different
Though all you are and you do seems exciting to me
That's why I wish to leave all I have here and follow you
Even if it seems a bit crazy I know

Just touches

My words or voice are never tender and subtle enough
To give you this that I wish to give you, my love
I just love your touches so much
That I will dream today, tonight
How it could be sweet to lie beside you still
And to feel all this what you give
Just when you are near

Please do not go

I need you
Somehow the right words stop flying in me
Just tears
Please do not leave me
Please
You say you need to be my only man
You afraid the same as me
That something could come between us
That's why we say some things
Just to make sure our selves
That we can't lose this
What we have, yes we have
Something so good
Please stay, my love
Why these tears came again
Why I'm so afraid
All the time
That you could go
Even when you say that you love
But you are so wonderful
And I'm so small
So unsure of this world
And me in it somehow
I'm just stealing smiles from each while that comes
Suddenly
I do not have any plan
For me here on this ground
Yes I wish justto drown in your arms
For good
But we both know
That this is not enough
We all have to find this way we wish to go
Before
I feel I'm on the way to nowhere
If I only lose my smile to go one
And my faith that I'm strong enough
To be worth of you
My beautiful.

I feel love

Hungry piece it was a bit
I admit
Though not current any more
Darling
I feel good
Yes so good
Having you
So smiling
Yes all is fine here
Yes I know
We gonna make it real
Soon
Yes soon
I'll touch you
Wonderful

You bring the nicest things to me

Each time you are coming here
You say something beautiful to me
As about this planning play recently
With us within
And it's like a birth for new dreams
To go on to cherish
But me ...
I have sometimes so many dark thoughts
So all that was clear and so good
Turns into the storm of feelings and weaknesses
I have within me
Then I fee , god what I'm doing here and why
Do I love him
Have to stop all this but it's too late
I shared all that was running through me
And again I made you confused or worried a bit
And this way I worry even more
And all is in my head
What is it for?
If there is nothing but love to enjoy?
So silly girl I'm at times
I wish you to forgive me
Once again
And let's go on
This dream we have
And let's be happy together
As we are
My love, my man
How I wish to kiss you again

Whenever

Whenever I go to you or you to me
I promise and
I always wish to keep
My legs wide open for you
Then bend over to show you my ass
Just ready
To make you feel this base primal need
To fuck me
Deep
Yes my man, I love it!

Yes do it please

I have a need inside me
I wish you to watch my hole
From behind
And touch it by your finger
Carefully
Letting it flow with fresh juices to taste
And then I wish you to smack it
Yes lick your finger now and put it again
Yes
I need you to watch me there
With your eyes open wide and your horny smile
I'm your bitch right now!
And I need you so much
I need you to be hard
Do not stop playin , please
Push it deeper
Oh yes!
And say that I'm your whore!
Yes I'm!
My love, please come inside, now
I want to feel your cock, wow
Yes
Oh yes!
My love!
My man!
Yes
Fuck me like this
Yes
Baby!
Please

For you I am

I love the way I'm for you
Oh so free it is, so natural
I love as I'm right now
Just can't stand a thought
That you could
Leave
Or think bad of me
Then all this starts
Darkness among the stars
I try to reach all the time
In your mind
In your heart
I drawn there
And I go
From years
So, please
Don't be afraid
To not have me
For you only

Yes beautiful but with you only

Yes you showed me the world
I wish to stay in for good
Though without you
It's just an empty space
Nothing more
Landscape as all other around
Yes beautiful
But can find nicer
Everywhere I suppose
But with you
With you...
This is all
I dreamt about
With your songs, with your smile, your care
Your spirit, your passionate soul and your heart
Just wish you to be near always and in love
To feel your hand in mine
To hear your voice
I wish to live with you like this
And I know that
I won't need anything else
I just wish to stay attractive to you as you are for me
And create still our own beautiful world
To live within
Each day each night that we share
Yes, sometimes we can go outside too
To eat or dance or doing something else
But here is always more
This our together world
I wish to keep and to enjoy
Forever

Sometimes I think that there is no more exciting place in this world than my own home oh maybe except this little tour through London when you are with me, in this small room, in the cinema and in the train and the restaurant when you put a part of your meal on my plate to let me taste it, oh god how sweet you are the lover of mine. I stop worry from today about anything, just wait. What ever comes will be good, I'm sure.

My treasure

My treasure
You
This one
Whom I'm afraid to lose
Each day
I know I shouldn't
Come what may
I'll just keep my place
In your heart
I know that

Not all in one time

I love in you even this
That you show me your self
Piece by piece

You never hurry up with all
Except these moments
When we are together
As one

Mist

After each wrong step
I make here
And I feel I lost a little bit
Of this
That I gained
Before
Or when all art between us
Splashed in plenty little pieces
I wish to learn
This love
From the start
I wish you to teach me
How to speak
To you
To bring you back here

For now
I'm lost in the mist
That your soul
Flows into my own
How to speak to you

Now?

How?

Or maybe just a touch can be a cure

I hope
My love

I hope
That
You will be there
Again
As I wish, as I want, as I need
Please, be there
My dear

Your sweet little messages

Your sweet little messages
I love them
They always alight me
Until another empty day comes
When there is no you enough
I love your I'm sorry's too
Even when there is nothing
I could be angry for
But you are so cute
To say you are sorry
That you were away
From me
Then I know
I see
That you care
Still
And I can live and I can smile
Just all is good and fine
And you are mine
As I'm yours
Nothing has changed
Nothing at all
My love

That train

I wish to be in that train
Which takes us to our room again
To feel this heat and longing in my veins
To hide my self in your arms, palms, mouth
And drown drown drown

Feed

I can't do or write anything special
So I'm sitting happy at home
You came last night
And you were so cute
I love your plans for the future too
I love all you say and you wish to do
For now
Only dreams fill me
I know it's a bit hopeless still
But can't do anything else
I'm just too happy
To move
I need only you
Inside for good

Not poetry

I'm not sure if I've been written any single poem so far
Perhaps all I've done is nothing but intimate conversation
That I shouldn't show at all
But what is poetry if not simple love and all its emotions
Captured in words ?
Just to show a bit this beauty we can hide from time to time
When we feel it when we are in love?
I couldn't write any single word
Without you, don't you know?
But sharing it yes it's a kind of crime
I just love it somehow
Kill me if you wish
But do not leave
Please

Unspoken beautiful words

I love all these never unspoken billion words
That you wish to share with me but you do not,
I know that all of them are beautiful and special and cute
I remember how sweet are your thoughts and voice
I can create another billion sweet conversations between us
and never say any word so beautiful as yours
And this that stays between these lines
which we were able to share sometimes

Poet

I know the man
Who is ready to eat your body
Deep
Just to write another piece
Of poetry
About the special taste of this
That he found
Inside it
Be Aware
Poets are everywhere

The thing about the places

Where is the centre of the world?

When?
Right now?

Pen St
Of course
So easy to catch
In Google earth
All ways lead
To you now
And the road is magical
So sweet to follow
So easy to fly and dream and smile
You are there
You are

Belt!

what ever your answer is
it always puts a smile on my face
I call it love
and I'm grateful

but are you sure?

belt not rope?

my love?

Days here

feed and happy
is there anything more I can say?
waiting
walking
eating
sucking
smiling
screaming
whispering
fucking
loving

the city is wonderful
what station are we at now?
forget the name again

Still dream world

There is still so little you
In my life
And even when I touch you
For a while
This all seems so unreal
Like no time for us still
We have place, public space
Little corner for new dreams
Nothing else
Two lives, real days, separate ways
And me so suddenly here
Stopped in time
In this magical beautiful crowded world
Though not mine
What can I do here?
Why did I come?
Oh yes for these few smiles, messages, charms
For you inside my arms
And to come back
Where, home?
I don't know
Yes I know
One home is real still
Another is a dream
But I'm so glad that you came to
Live here my sweet unreal man
As long as you wish
As long as you can
Forever perhaps
Who knows
We love to believe such words
I know
So let's believe
And dream dream dream
We are both good in this
I think

At least you stay inside me

So you are going to have your life now
Not ours
For some time you say
Four or ten years
Yes, time goes quickly
Meanwhile we have our little dream
Clever boy
And I know that perhaps
It's best like this
To leave things as they are
And just wait

It's just sometimes
I have enough
This never ending
Waiting room
That my life seems to be
From the start to the end
It's a little bit sad but no
I do not complain
I do understand
It's just reality again...
Any way
You are everything what I have inside me
This I wont leave
This I can keep
And this is sweet

Don't say silly things like this please

Oh yes
Sometimes a great sinner I am
Especially inside my mind
Which needs so much passions
New loves and smiles
It needs to be also so free and wild
At times
But do not take all I write
So directly please
It's more longings, desires and dreams in it
Than this what really happen to me
Besides you can't so simply find new mum
For children we have
Don't be ridiculous
Mum is only one here having break for few days
So don't say silly things like this
It makes me sick
I'm coming home soon
To them if not for you
And the journey I can say was good
Had time enough to realise few things too
Had time to know a bit more
Which way to go
Just don't say silly things
Like this
please
But you have a right to be worried a bit I admit

This play here starts to be more sensitive
and the line between reality and dream
Seems to be really thin
From the time you came on the scene
but the show must go on
I don't see any reason to stop
I do enjoy this plot

No time for love

You know what I'm thinking now?
That you simply don't have the time
For any lover in your life
It's just as I
When I'm home doing all this stuff I belong to
So all it was very nice dream
You and me
But simply not real
In the situation we are in
But it's nice to know that you love me
I love you too
Well good bye for now

Just keep inside this what we find

So through these days
I just found out
That I still can't count on you
Mostly you fail
Just sometimes no
What is always so nice surprise
I can say
Besides yes
You are this special person
I love to be close to
And share each thought
Even when you can't answer at all

From other things I know now
I do not long anymore
For this big change
All is so similar actually
Just crowd around can be less or more
Just few places to look
make some slight difference
But all this can't change the fact
That all you really have is inside

All places seem to be more available each day
Global world seems so small
Dreams are no longer so difficult to gain
So you have to look something else

What really matters
Well as always is love
Do we have it
Do we have it
My love?
Can we care for it enough?
Is there any chance for us
To survive like that?

Maybe better not think of all this
Let's still share our lives our dreams
As we do so far as we need
Let's be together the way we can
It is a good thing at the end
No matter what anyone can say
It's a rare thing so let's keep it
inside
Yes it's a good place for us
The only one we can have
I guess

Goodbye for real

I love you yes but I think that
I can't be with a man
Who fails just too many times
On whom I can't rely
For whom I'm on the last place
Things to care or persons important to not
Disappoint
I know that at least
You are always so sweet at the end
The best thing I have ever had
But you are cause of so many tears
Doubts fears
That everything can just disappear
That everything is not real

Or I just wish too much
Or it's just not the right time
I don't really know
Just too many broken promises
You give

Maybe it's my fault
Maybe I shouldn't come here at all
To give you so many chances
To not come or not to do
What I had hoped you would
What you love to promise me
But all promises are so hard to keep
So nothing is as it should be
But it's just life you can say
Yes yet still too many broken promises
Too many times I'm losing a ground for a while
Too many times I have to wait
in vain
I try yes I try to understand
But it's too much to stand
Take it easy you can say
Yes I can
And it's not a problem to me to consist in my self yes
But this way alone I'm still not with you
Don't you understand this
No I think you don't
I just expect too much I know
So dream is not a dream anymore
Is it love?
Just life and the way we treat each other
Yes I love you still
I'm just afraid it can't survive the time

And the way it goes now
Make me just unsure
How it could be for real one day
You make me so sad ignoring fooling me still
Yes your sorrows are sweet after all
But for life is just not enough
You are cause too many tears and doubts

Yes besides all this you are beautiful
Charming, sweet, wild and good
But I need the man I can rely on
And I can't lose my ground
So many times a day
I don't have force enough
To such life as you offer me right now
Yes you are an exciting type
I can't deny
You give me so much so good things
Without you I feel so empty yes
But to live together is just not enough

But thank you for all
All these sweet moments you gave to me
This instantaneous care too
I really appreciate that you say you love
And some moments with you I never forget
My beautiful lover
My dream, my secret
I'll keep you inside me forever
But for now I have to say good bye
There is no chance to live together for real
We always knew this I think
We just loved to forget about this for a while
But I think it's time to wake up
Let's keep us as a dream from now
And forget about any real life
We do not belong here
To be together like this
We always knew this I think
I was just fooling my self
But I can no longer
Goodbye
My sweet beautiful impossible man

Wolfie lover

My wolf came into the forest
To take me
It's not the first time
Not the last one
He does so

Maybe because I love this
Quite inconspicuous smile
He has just between one and another

Feast of him
By me

My sunny

You are still able
To make me
so happy
By a single word
My beautiful

Your call

You let me do bad things my beloved
I know you enjoy these sweet little crimes
Which flow from your to my soul
To raddle us together for good
In the secret
We can't share with anyone
Flair mind you are
And I can't say no
When I love
So we go
Together
Low
Right now

Are you still hungry?

Yes you can do it
With passion
Your special inner charm
Beautifully and strong
With all this that you can give
So naturally to me
But if there is no real care
For today for us
You know
It seems a bit sad
After all
And I become calm
Wishing less
I just wait
Now
I learn
To live
Separately
For months
For years
Maybe
Is this patience good
For this love?
Can passion survive
In hibernation?
Well we will see
My belove
Are you still hungry
As you were before?

Lookout

You answer
My inner questions
Like you are living
Inside me
You know the best I need
You are waiting
On your golden branch
Keeping lookout on me
still
Touching dreams
This mad atmosphere
between
Alluring
Inspiring
Sweet

I like you here

Drifting

Yes I love all these
Sweet little stops
Swimming in your mind creations
When I imagine myself as this mermaid
Who sings for you
Another song
Leading you to a secret death
That you could drown once again
In this irresistible charm
Of immortal belife
That we can wake up
Again
Just to dream
To get lost
One more time

The circle of our needs never ends
So we are here
Again and again
Having hope for more

That is how it goes
That is how I love

You here

This never-ending story

Hey you - the Lover
I know you exist for me
Only when you feel that I need this
So don't think
I forget about you now
I just know
That we have the time still
So I wait
And play here
You know how I love this world
My waiting room
Is still full of dreams about you

Question

There is a silence
On your site
When I don't write
Why?

Traveling in your mind

You seem angry a bit
Being now a piece of this dream
Used in a bad way perhaps
Waiting still for scaps
To serve back
Your wonderful mind
Created for my pleasure
Right now
Yes I love to live here
Inside you
And mix you and him
Do what you want now
I'm not afraid
I enjoy your part
and I'm glad
to find you

Chair

I like when you do so
I mean
This little move of the chair
Which you put near mine
To come closer a bit

Just some little smile
During a long day
You bring
By your fresh touch
of new story
That could start
Between
Us
Perhaps
At least
inside
Our minds

My own wolf

I wonder
Where is my wolf now
Is he hunting still
So busy with a new dream to gain?
Or with all these things around him?
To arrange, to catch, to keep?

I love to imagine his life still
Even if it is so closed to me here
I do not belong to this forest he own
I know
So I do what I want
In my own world
He will come again
One day
Wolves like to be free
But this one still belongs to me
It's so sweet
When I am sure

Time, place, words
Doesn't matter anymore
When we know
What we know

Who you are

You are just the right home
For my thoughts
To explode

You are the mirror
I can see
The right pictures
Of my own dreams in
So you mix
Living here
Being the part
Of my own way
Through the light
Is it bad for you?
Is it hard?

No reason

It's just our writing that we share
We both long for their fingertips
(maybe you long for something else
more)

So, wandering among sweet dreams
or last pleasures
We meet here suddenly
Two souls in need
Which understand each other perfectly

Just to spend some time here
No names, no faith
Simple thoughts
To check
And to send something back
No reason
For this

but wish, a little spark
among the dark
or among all other sweet things we live with
It is good
To be here
With you
and your writing too

Your loving fingers

They know so much
They know how to touch
They know how to push
They know how to rub
They know how to slip
They know how to keep
They know how to wander here and there
They know where to press
They know how to undress
They know how to caress
They know how to arouse me
They know how to make me scream
They know how to make me wet
They know how to make me wait
They know how to make me sweat
They know how to make me hungry too
They know how to make me asking more
They even know how to make me begging you to stop
They know how to make me dream on and on
They know how to make me soft
They know how to make me
The woman in love

They even know how to hurt me
Beautifully

Indeed
Loving fingers they are

Admired

Some

Some people we feel inside
No matter where they are

It's a miracle
Of life
It's what matters
And what you really have

Easy going

We do not complicate things
We just have a little bit more
Than we had before

I didnt know it's so easy
until we met

but now
I just smile
and wait
for the next
step

Meeting

I met a woman today
She said she doesnt like any man
Why so I asked?
They hurt her and treat her badly
Don't know details
They think we are only
a sex machine, she said too
Well hard to believe somehow...
Besides we both like this game
And if we know
How to make things hot
I can't find this really bad
We can feel if someone treats us
The way we wish or not
I suppose...
But maybe I'm wrong

At the end she said
That I talk as a man
Well it's ok...

So I make angels from you?
Yes I make you beautiful for me
And then I enjoy
How good
Is all this we do from now

So I'm the man
In this woman's eyes
bizzard

Come my angel soon
I miss you

and don't forget to show your tusks
a bit

You know

I like it

At least

Even missing you badly at times
I feel good
When I know
That you are with me still
At least
Within your dreams

Colour

I'm not that noisy
As I used to be
You should know though
I still love you
As I did before

I just like this silence now
somehow

You who wait for words

I know you are waiting
But I have others
To feed up at the moment

For now

I love when you are there
Missing me
Leaving your sweet little traces
In our spaces

Then I know
That this journey through the moon
Will be continued

And don't say sorry
That you came
too late

You are always welcome
Even when I'm away

Just be
near
connected to my soul
as always
as you were before
It's enough
for now

Drop a hint

It's not so important
Who you are generally
More important is
Who you are for me
Actually

So be as "nice" as I wish
Please

and don't forget
To be your self
In it
Still

Almost without you

Daily sadness and joys
Captured my soul suddenly
It's almost like you were not here
Anymore
Just sometimes this scream inside
Come back, come back
I really need you to live beside me
I need this hope
For more to go on
What ever I have to do right now
Right here
To live day by day
To not die
Inside
Without this special you
This dream too
This love

Once upon a time

You didn't come then
You had a busy night for sure
My message wasn't tempting enough
I know
So we missed again
Days are mine
Yours are nights
There is no space for us
So the only thing that keeps us together
Is this sweet memory
Of touch, of voice, of love
We made once a upon a time
In a sunny day, in a glorious night
In the city somewhere on the ground
How sweet memory to keep is this
How nice
But what now?
Wait wait of course
We still have the time for this love
We still cannot rush too fast
So we have what we have
Long hours, days, years to wait
Yes
By the way
Will you come this time
As you said?
Or should I forget?

You and me

We know
How to hurt
Each other
Perfectly
Then we wait
To come back
Then we feel
This delight
And this need
To be right here

Don't leave

You must be blind
To not see
How my heart
Is bleeding
When you say so
When you are leaving
You say it's me who hurt
Look at me now
Don't you see my tears?
Don't leave
Don't leave
Please

you

No you are not a gentle type
Of husband
Don't cheat your self
You are a rascal
And I want you this way
I'm your whore
And we belong to each other

And we feel well
Don't we?

You are back

You belong to my internal world
My beautiful madness, my wonderful
What can be stronger than this?
More inspiring, more sweet?
We just have to go deeper now
There is no way out
From here
You know this, my dear
It can hurt at times I know
We are as we are
And this is our love
Lust, obsession whatever you call it
But this links us forever
Because we enjoy it
Because we live here
And because it's rare
Happy I'm again
I know you too
We belong here for good
Yes my love
So good you are back
Inside my world
And you smile
I know you smile right now
Just as me because you are
Back in to my heart

Abandoned

My darling feels abandoned
What to do
He lives lit by my passion
Another way his silence kills
The rest of me
Drifting slowly on the surface
Of my delirious dream

When he dies I do too
Yet I can't run anymore
Don't have force in me enough
To chase this dream
With the same flame

The key

You are so delightful a part of my life
All pieces are just as important
I can't explain it
I can only enjoy it
And go on my way
Watching, feeling love
The key
Is the beauty
And the way
To follow

So much love around

Until

Sometimes I can feel like your heart stopped beating
When I keep silence and the distance is killing this dream
But when I'm back and think of you more
I can see there is still you here
For me

I love to come back to you
I love it
and I will
Until you let me
Be near
Until I can feel
You want me still

It's just how it is

And what do you think there
Being silent
I'm always curious
How far we can go
From each other
For how long

And it's me who breaks this silence still
It's just how it is
With you and me

I know you wait
And I know you can go
When you don't feel me
Enough
It's just how it is
With you and me

I know this

Still

You are the last person I talk to
Yet still the closest one
My beloved

Reading you

You are so cute
With this love in your words
Not important so much
It's for me
Or someone else
You look beautiful
With this special clothes
On your soul
You look good
And I like
Watching you now
So stay like this
For me please
Be so sweet
Inspiring
neat...
I adore it

The circle of run

All of you wish the same
Then
When one is successful
You become disappointed a bit
For a moment
Then you want more
To run for it
To try at least
To win

How it's sweet
The circle of life
The beginning and the end
To start again
To keep, to lost
And rebuild
And go on
Still

Today

Today
I just drowned again
In this blissful warm assurance
Which my heart gives to me
That I love you
Indeed
Forever
So sweet
What ever comes
What ever may be

and I'm happy

Angelique

I long
This life
At times
As you had
Angelique
So merveilleuse
So sweet

On the way

Direction is one
From the start to the end
Just this space between
Can be enjoyable less or more
Just the number of thoughts, actions,
Meetings, things you have done
Is different for everyone
Just the way you are
and love or hate
This world
Makes some difference
I suppose

What do you really want
Right now?

We were lovers

Nothing can go wrong
I'm sure it won't
We have to believe just
We have to go on
And laugh and cry
and Love
Together

Complexive

You want me to be yours
But not with you now
You want me to be a whore
And a saint of course
Never look for another man
or yes I can
In your fantasies
I can fuck them all
Just to turn you on
And me
Yes it's sweet of you
I have a right to pleasure
I have a right to smile
I have a right to dance
as you wish as you play
when you came here
to look
then all is broken again
then you feel hurt and me
complexive nature
don't you like this?
I think you do
So it's broken now
Of course
but you say you will miss me
you will I am sure
and I will
That's how is it
We can't do anything

It's love which is perfect not we

Do we have to be perfect
To love?
Always true to each other always good
I don't think so
It's love which is perfect for us
To catch each moment it comes
Each smile, longing, desire
Is love possible to get for good?
I don't know this yet
Instead
I know how it is
To have it inside
And smile with it and cry
And live and fly
And go on, break sometimes too or lost
Or love more than one
It's so floating sometimes

Yes but some stay for good
At least inside our soul
I call it the miracle
I call it sweet love
I hide it or I show
Depends, the time is always a part of it
And me and dreams too and memories of course
And life goes on from one to another corner
From one to another love
The circle again the way to follow
We never know we will stay or we have to go
We can come back too, I am sure
All depends on the flow and us and what we want
And how we can see each other
As always the same, I know...

But it's how it goes
With me and you
Let's fly let's love
Whatever it is
It doesnt matter at all
No definitions we need
To enjoy what we can have in this world.

Constant stay

Once upon a time
Heraclit said:
"panta rej"
and yes I believe this old truth too
I can see how time changes all

but you
please
constant stay
for me
I wish this
and I dream still
of you and me
together forever
just like this
so beautiful so sweet
sometimes wild too
and in love

so please
stay like this for me
and believe

The miracle

What are you looking for?
The miracle

Why so?
Because everything else I think I know now

Yes I am yours

Men sometimes like
To give themselves to me
They write down on the letters they send
"I am yours"
I never send them back the same
And they know I am just a bird
They can't catch
And they let me fly

But I always come back
To the nest of your heart
And I love to hear
Your words

"You are mine"

Yes I am
And I love to be
Your woman

You were here
So you were here again
With your hunger
For more words
From me
Or other fluids
So sweet

I like when our worlds mix
I like to be
In your dreams
or wishes too

They are fine
Delicious and wild
As you

Neurotic

I am still afraid
There is too much of me here
And my words can touch you too much
Or that there is not enough love I show to you
And you can go away
or that you simply can't stand
all this what I make around
or that you stop believe
in you and me
Together

Why so full of fears is still
between you and me
I can't explain

Truth

I am never untrue
In my heart or words of love
To you

Maybe sometimes
I just hide
One lover or few

To not upset you
That's all

Network

Each day it's more hard
To find anything special outside
Just some strangers or people you can smile to and say hello
Most of the time nothing more
Maybe at times you pass someone
You like this special way too
And you create another story of love
Between you both which never grow up
To something real
Maybe sometimes you try
To have some kind of meetings too
And it seems you come closer
And something was born

But the real life
You have here
Your friends wait every day
All these special minds connected
In one story you live in
In your book in your dream world
And in your so special place
Where you can really be shameless open and true
You with all this what you really enjoy and love
What can be more exciting than this?
Nothing maybe a part of it in touch
Once for a year or more
Is it any difference by the way?
When you wait longer it taste even better
So you learn to be patient too
In mean time you have all this world
To enjoy

Love me please

You don't have to
do anything
Just love me
and try to understand
Please
Whatever you see
Whatever you hear
Don't stop
And believe

Next time

Next time when we meet
Don't say any word
Just take me
The way you do so
Wild hard strong free
I need this
my darling
so please
do this
to me

Don't stop

It's adventure time you said
To me
And you are right
and you know me well enough
To set me free
Right here
I love when you know
What to do
To make me yours
For good
And to let me love you more

You are only one man on this world
Who keeps me mad in love with you
For years
It's so good
You know?
It's so good
Don't stop

Layers

Some just can't see more layers
We all wear
so they see only this what can be seen
all the rest is disgusting and insane for them
be careful for people with walls in their head
they won't understand
they will be first to judge you
and to let you down
better to leave
fight doesn't have any sense
they have to discover their own boundaries themselves
you have nothing to do there
they won't understand
they are not ready yet
and you can only fail
you this open one
and insane
beautiful loser
But in their eyes
even not beautiful just mad
So free you are
in your own mind
stay like this
it's just another level
of understanding
of yourself
stay on your way
to heaven or to hell
you know that all is just a journey
and you can leave
or you can stay
for a while
depends on you and your will
you are the creator
of your destiny
and your dreams
you are here the one who lives your life
don't stop then
and go on your way
it's nothing you can do more
just go
you know what you feel the best
and you know what is right and what is wrong
In your case
you don't need poor advice
from people who don't know
your mind and your soul
they are not special to you at all

Little advice

Don't be too seriouse please
It's not sexy

A man

I think you are an adult man
You take all the blame on you
It's cute

Take a walk on the wild side

So you really love me like this baby
You are beautiful
And you know me so well

You know when to set me free
and keep me with you still

We did this darling

you see baby
at least
some of our dreams came true
we did things
that we do not wish to make with others

they are precious
and only for us
marvellous

Little important details of your personality and acts

Mostly these are
Very little things
Which makes you so great
In my eyes
At least

Our fantasy

Is that true darling
Is it just that we want what we cannot have?
So why do I already feel you in me
you with me here?

I know it's a bit like a fantasy or dream
but it's still
you and me in this

My sweet addition

Is it anything I need more than this writing to you my beloved?
Any alcohol, drug or even sex can't replace the real delight
Of my connection here mind to mind
I just have a little hope that you read me
And it's good for your ear
To hear my thoughts to stay here
So bared I am with them
So confusing or repeating sometimes
They will be never so beautiful
As all sweet signs of your presence
Beside me
But I need them to live
and to feel you here

Go if you want

Some can't understand this sweet madness of mine
which keeps me such a happy girl for years somehow
they think they can give me more
It's wrong all my joy is here
You can share it too
If you want but you can't take me away
To reality at all
Because I do not believe
In real life anymore
It's here my world
With my love

I don't need perfect lover

It's not a point to be so perfect lover at all
It's a bit more complicated
I am afraid
But how come you know it
It's the hidden part of the story

Not ready for love

I am such a bad girl how come you love me?
Sometimes when you wish to give too much
to the person who has not that much to offer to you,
you fail and this gift is just a heavy thing to keep

so you push it away
and you go your way
feeling guilty
just because he was so great to you and you wasn't
enough

One piece is gone

Music and pictures are gone
But I still have my words
And few friends around
And some dreams still alive
It's not so bad
yet

The reason

Hey you
It's just because I want you from very deep of my heart
I can be so open, free and wild
Don't you know that?

Relief

I know baby that we are both able to many things
We just don't have to do it
We don't have to
Do you feel relief now?
I do

I know why we went so far

I can explain you why
We went so far
Because we both like
Dancing on the thin line
Between heaven and hell
Inside our mind
That's why darling
But it's so good we know when to stop
Or rather you
Are this one who knows
But sometimes we have to
Try all what leads us to know more
About each other
Besides we had some fun with this
Don't you think?

Bittersweet taste of yours

No one is able to make me
Fight so many times
With my own shadows
To let me fail
With them again
Maybe that's why I love you so much?
I never know what the new day
Brings with you
You are so unforeseeable
But that's why so exciting too
And this journey
Through you and me is so amazing
And leads to dreams
And after war is always peace
So I can live still
And wait here
For more wonders, battles, smiles, tears
Whatever you bring to me
But I can't leave
It's too beautiful
And too sweet bitter too
But sweet the most
After all.

Flames

Why do you play with me like this baby
Why you force me to do things
You do not really enjoy after all
What do you want to know
How blind I am in this love?
Or how far I can go
Into madness?
Then you can leave
Being sure
I am not strong enough
To say no
I don't know
Maybe it's nothing but passion
Which leads you and me
And we don't really know
How it comes and where do we go
And we run and we burn
Until one feels hurt
And it's time to stop
For how long?

The end

It's all gone it's all gone
It's just you and me
Who stay here
Do not worry baby
Do not worry

But what we are going to do now?

www.ingramcontent.com/pod-product-compliance
Lightning Source LLC
LaVergne TN
LVHW021133080426
835509LV00010B/1345